ANIMAL HOMES

Angela Wilkes

KINGFISHER

Contents

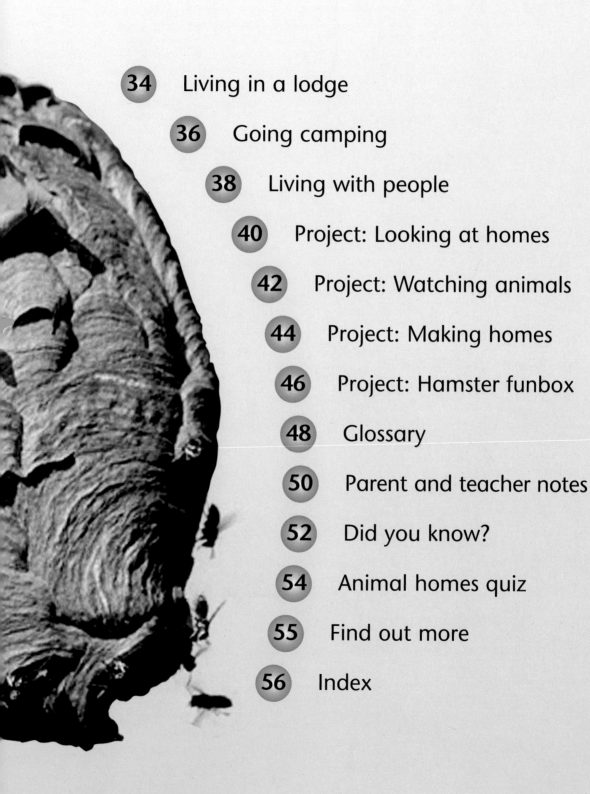

6 What is a home?

Animals need homes for all the same reasons that people do. Homes provide shelter and keep animals warm in winter. They are a safe place to rest and to bring up babies.

Hard to find

Animals build their homes out of materials that match their surroundings. This makes it hard for predators to spot them. ● ● ● ● ●

Safe place for babies

Homes such as this bird's nest are only built for bringing up babies. A nest is warm, snug and out of the reach of danger. This is where a mother bird lays her eggs and brings up her young.

Different homes

Animals make many kinds of homes. Some build nests, while others make dens, or dig burrows.

Living in a pond

Many different animals live in the still, fresh water of a pond. Here they can find good hiding places, and lots of things to eat.

Finding a mate
Newts live in ponds in the spring. They look for a mate, then lay their eggs in the water.

Blowing bubbles

The water spider spins a web between water plants. It then fills the web with air to make a bubble in which it can live.

Fatherly love

A male stickleback sticks plants together to make a nest. A female lays her eggs in the nest and the male fans fresh water over them with his fins.

Keeping damp

Amphibians, such as frogs and toads, live in damp, shady places. They need to keep their skin moist and slimy. Some make their homes in unusual spots.

Living in a hole

When it rains, the water-holding frog's skin soaks up water. The slime on its skin sets to make a cocoon that keeps the water in. The frog then burrows into the sand to escape the desert heat.

water-holding frog

Treetop homes

Strawberry poison-dart frogs live in steamy rainforests. They hide from the hot sun in pools of rainwater that collect in the middle of huge plants.

Burrowing toads

Spadefoot toads dig burrows and spend most of their time there. But when it rains, they come above ground to find a mate.

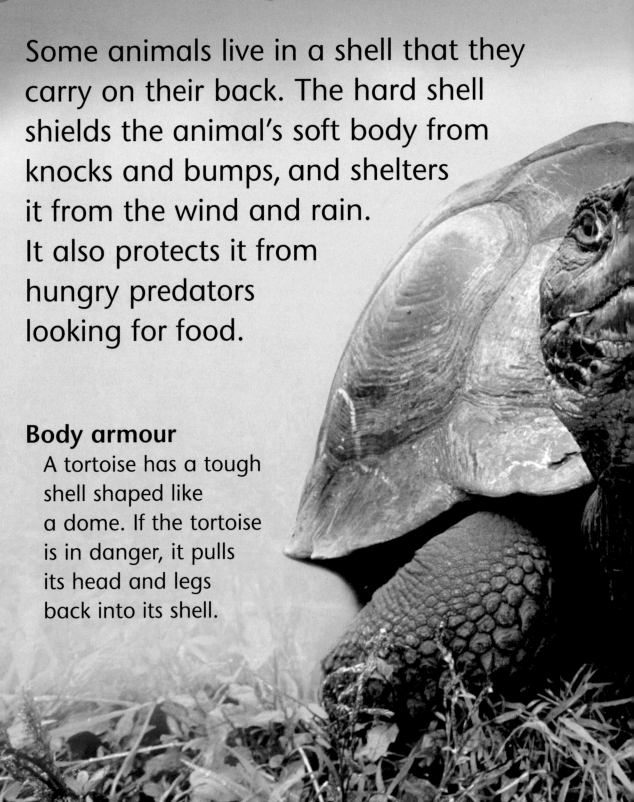

Mobile homes

Some animals live in a shell that they carry on their back. The hard shell shields the animal's soft body from knocks and bumps, and shelters it from the wind and rain. It also protects it from hungry predators looking for food.

Body armour

A tortoise has a tough shell shaped like a dome. If the tortoise is in danger, it pulls its head and legs back into its shell.

A home that grows

As a snail grows,
its shell grows too,
so the shell is always just
the right size. Snails slink
back inside their shells
to hide from danger.

Borrowed home

A hermit crab has no hard
shell of its own, so it finds
an empty mollusc shell and
moves in. When the hermit
crab grows, it moves to
a bigger shell.

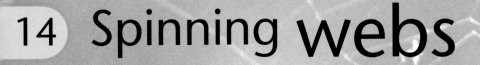

Spinning webs

Most spiders spin webs to catch insects. They build them out of silk threads from their own bodies. But some spiders live in other types of home, such as holes or burrows.

Cobweb trap
The orb spider spins a beautiful sticky web between the stems of plants. The spider lies in wait for insects in the centre of the web, or hides under a nearby leaf.

Under a rock

Some spiders make nests in hollows under rocks. They line the nest with thick silk and lay their eggs. Then they wait to pounce on passing insects.

Ambush!

The trapdoor spider digs a tunnel and lines it with silk. Then it makes a lid on top, like a trapdoor. The spider hides in the tunnel and darts out to catch prey.

Where **birds live**

Birds build nests so they have a warm, safe place to lay their eggs and look after their chicks. Most birds' nests are in trees, but some are on steep cliffs or even on the ground.

Hanging nest
The penduline tit hangs its purse-shaped nest from a twig. It is lined with soft wool and fluff from reeds or catkins to make a cosy home for the female and babies.

Fancy work

A male cape weaver bird weaves a complicated oval nest out of grass and reeds. The only way in is through a short tunnel at the bottom. This helps to protect it from predators.

Hungry chicks

Chicks hatch in their nest. They are helpless and cannot leave. They open their beaks wide to beg for food.

wasp larva in a cell

Cell homes

Wasps and bees build fantastic nests, made up of lots of tiny cells. Young wasps and bees can grow up safely in these little compartments.

Laying eggs

A queen wasp lays one egg in each cell. Each egg will become a wasp larva. Older wasps look after the eggs and larvae.

Paper home

A wasp's nest is made of layers of paper around the larvae cells. The wasps make paper by chewing up wood and mixing it with their spit.

Moving house

Bees live and work together. When bees need a new home, they fly away in a huge group called a swarm.

Honeycomb homes

Bees' nests are called hives. Inside a hive are wax honeycombs made of lots of cells. The cells hold honey or a baby bee.

leafcutter ants

Living in a colony

Most ants and termites live in huge groups called colonies. They work together to build enormous nests in which to raise their young.

Food for the colony

Leafcutter ants live in rainforests. They bite off pieces of leaf and carry them back to their nest. They store the leaves in special gardens and a fungus grows on them, making a tasty food for the ants.

queen termite

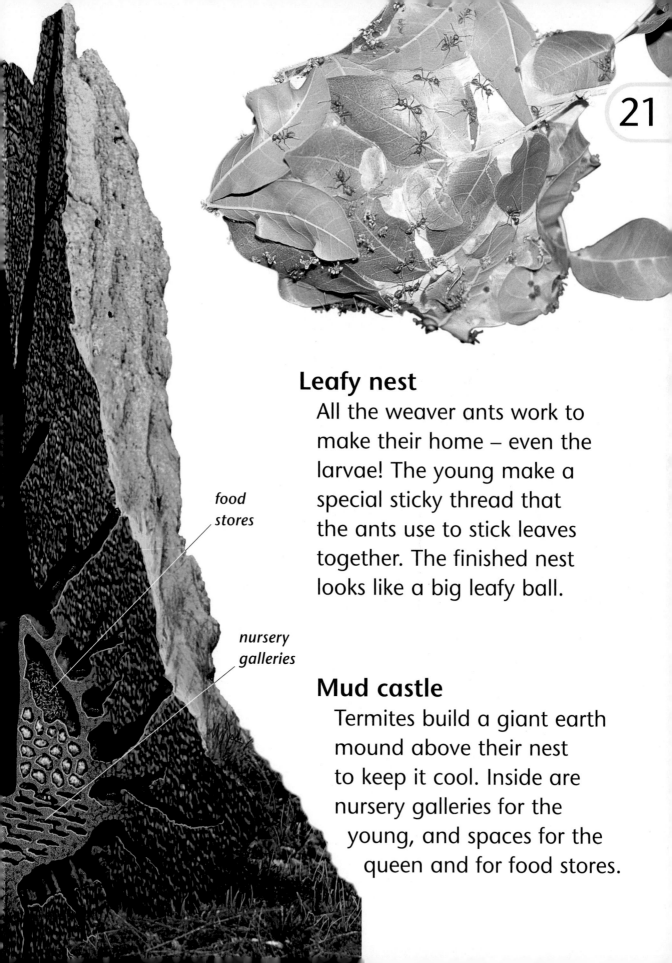

food
stores

nursery
galleries

Leafy nest

All the weaver ants work to make their home – even the larvae! The young make a special sticky thread that the ants use to stick leaves together. The finished nest looks like a big leafy ball.

Mud castle

Termites build a giant earth mound above their nest to keep it cool. Inside are nursery galleries for the young, and spaces for the queen and for food stores.

22 Mini homes

Mice live in lots of places. Some live in fields and some live in woods. Others even live in people's houses. But all mice build nests to rest in and bring up their babies.

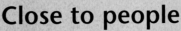

Close to people

House mice make their nests from shredded paper, old rags or grass. They always build them in a small hiding place well out of sight.

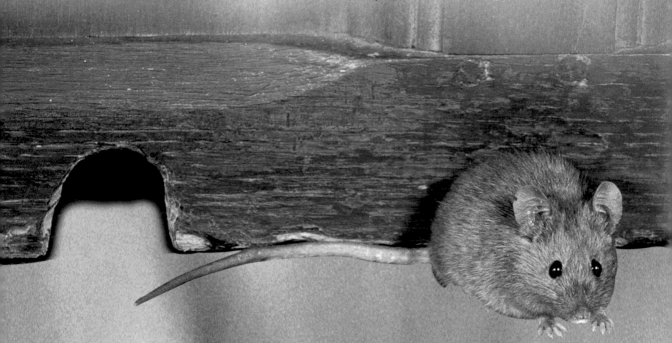

Grassy homes

The tiny harvest mouse lives in tall grass. It weaves strips of grass around plant stems to make a snug, round nest.

Sleepy mouse

In the autumn, the dormouse makes a cosy nest out of shredded bark. Then it curls up into a ball and goes to sleep for the long, cold winter.

Under the ground

Marmots live high in the mountains. When the first winter snows fall, the whole family moves into a big burrow lined with grass, and goes to sleep.

Fast asleep

The marmots block the entrance to the burrow with rocks and soil to stop predators getting in. Then they snuggle together for warmth, and hibernate until spring comes again.

Where dogs live

Foxes and dingoes are wild dogs. They make their homes by digging dens in soft earth, or by taking over and enlarging the homes of other animals. Dens provide shelter from the hot sun or cold weather, and are a safe place to bring up pups.

Desert homes
Kit foxes live in stony deserts in North America. They sleep in their dens during the day, when the sun is at its hottest. At night, when it is cooler, they go out hunting.

Ready-made den
Dingoes live in Australia.
When a mother dingo
is about to have
pups, she moves
into a safe den.
This is often a
big hole beneath
tree roots or
some rocks.

Living in the snow

Polar bears live in the snowy Arctic. When they are tired, they dig a shallow pit in the snow, and sleep in it. In the autumn, a pregnant polar bear digs a den in a snowdrift. This is where she will spend the long, dark winter.

Snow babies

The mother bear stays in the den until the spring. In the early winter, she gives birth to one or two cubs. She feeds them her milk, and they all sleep for most of the winter.

Leaving the den

In the spring, the polar bear and her young come out of the den. The mother is very hungry as she has not eaten all winter. She takes her cubs on to the sea ice, where she can hunt for food.

Going batty

Bats go out hunting for food at night and rest during the day. They do not make special homes, but roost in trees, caves, barns or even attics.

Leafy shelter

Fruit bats live in huge groups called colonies and roost in tall trees by day. They hang upside down from branches, clinging on tightly with the claws on their feet. Then they wrap their skinny wings around themselves for protection.

Dark caves

Many bats sleep in large caves.
Thousands of them roost upside down,
packed closely together. When
evening comes, the bats set out
to feed. Some bats feed on
insects. Others, like these
flying foxes, eat fruit and
the nectar from flowers.

Riverside
homes

dragonfly

Many animals live on the banks of rivers and streams. Here they are close to fresh water, and there are plenty of plants, small creatures and fish to eat. They are also safely out of the reach of most predators.

Water babies

Adult dragonflies live beside rivers. The larvae live in the water. When the larvae are ready to become adults, they climb up a plant's stem. Their skin splits open along their backs, and the adult dragonfly climbs out.

Nest tunnel

Kingfishers dig a tunnel in a soft river bank. At the end of the tunnel, the female kingfisher makes a small chamber and lays her eggs. When the chicks hatch, she brings them fish to eat.

Rest burrows

Platypuses live near lakes and rivers. A mother platypus digs a long nesting burrow in the soft earth of the bank. Here, she lays her eggs and looks after her babies.

Living in a lodge

Beavers are clever builders. They construct dams across streams to make ponds. Then they build homes, called lodges, in the middle of these ponds.

Safe from enemies

The beavers line the lodge with dry grasses to keep it snug and warm. All the entrances are under water, safe from predators.

Timber!

Using their sharp front teeth, beavers can cut down trees. They gnaw around the bottom of a tree until it falls down. Then they chew pieces off to make small logs.

Saving food for later

Beavers only eat plants. They store some food at the bottom of the pond, so they can eat all winter.

Going camping

Big apes, such as chimpanzees,
orang-utans and gorillas, do not
have one home. They move
from place to place.
At night, they
make leafy nests
and camp out.

Climbing trees

Chimpanzees make tree
nests at night-time. They
bend leafy branches over
to make comfortable beds
on which they can sleep.

Leafy nests

Orang-utans make two tree nests
a day. They make a small nest for
a nap and at night, they build
platforms in the forks of trees.

Heavy sleepers

Female gorillas nest in
trees. Male gorillas
make nests on
the ground, as
they are too
heavy to
sleep in trees!

Living with people

Towns and cities offer shelter, food and warmth. As they have grown in size, more animals have moved into them. Animals often settle into new homes in the most surprising places.

Cardboard bed

In North America, raccoons have moved to town gardens and even into city centres. They live in attics and sheds. Raccoons eat almost anything, and even help themselves to food from dustbins.

Living the high life

The peregrine falcon usually lives on cliff or rock faces. In cities, it roosts on churches, tower blocks and even radio masts.

Chimney-pot homes

For hundreds of years, the white stork has nested close to people. It makes its huge nest on top of chimneys and houses. Some people build special platforms for storks to nest on.

Looking at homes

You will need
- Plastic cup
- Scissors
- Plastic food wrap
- Elastic bands

Make a pond viewer
With this simple underwater viewer you can take a closer look at the small creatures that live in ponds and streams.

1

Hold the plastic cup firmly in one hand. Then hold the scissors in your other hand and carefully cut out the bottom of the cup.

2

Cut out a large circle of plastic food wrap. Stretch it tightly over the cut end of the cup, until the food wrap is smooth.

3

Stretch a couple of elastic bands over the food wrap to hold it in place. Pull the edges of the plastic food wrap tight again.

4

To use the pond viewer, dip the end covered with food wrap into the water. Then look through the open end at the top of the cup.

Make a nest

Watch different birds making their nests in spring. See if you can copy them by making a bird's nest of your own.

You will need
- Paint brush and glue
- Plastic bowl
- Dried grass
- Moss
- Feathers and leaves
- Sweet wrappers

Using a paint brush, spread glue all around the outside of the bowl. Pick up small handfuls of dried grass and stick them to the bowl.

Spread glue around the inside of the bowl. Then stick on a layer of more dried grass and moss, to make a soft, cosy middle.

Scatter a few small feathers and leaves inside the nest to make it look realistic. Decorate with a few sweet wrappers to add colour.

Watching animals

Make a teepee hide

If you make a simple teepee in your garden or local park, you can hide inside it and watch animals.

You will need
- Large sheet
- 4 bamboo canes
- Garden twine
- Paint brush
- Scissors
- Poster paints

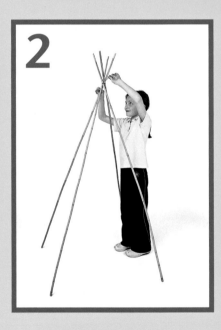

1 Mix the paints with a little water, so they are easy to use. Paint circles and other bold shapes on the sheet. Leave the sheet to dry.

2 Stand the four bamboo canes together and make them into a teepee shape. Cut a long piece of twine and tie the canes together firmly at the top.

3

Wrap the sheet around the teepee frame. Tie it in place at the top of the canes with more twine.

4

See where your face comes up to on the sheet. Cut out a peep hole big enough for you to see out of.

5

Go inside the teepee hide and close the loose edges of the sheet behind you. Keep as quiet and still as you can and wait to see which animals come close. Take a notebook and pencil so you can make notes of what you see.

Making homes

Make a hermit crab
Make a crab out of modelling clay and put it in an empty shell. Then it will be just like a real hermit crab.

You will need
- Shell
- Modelling clay
- Pipe-cleaner

Roll two pieces of modelling clay into balls for the crab's head and body. Make four small sausages for legs and two claw shapes.

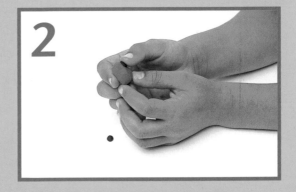

Break off two tiny pieces of a different colour modelling clay. Roll them into little balls for the eyes, and stick them on to the head.

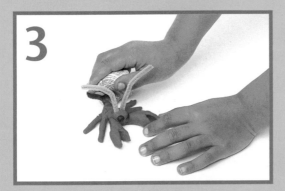

Stick the head, claws and legs to the crab's body. Make feelers from two bits of pipe-cleaner, then put the crab in the shell.

Flowerpot home

Make a flowerpot home for minibeasts. Check to see what is inside it every day, and draw the creatures you find there.

You will need
- Flowerpot
- Small rock
- Notebook and pen

Ask an adult to help you find a shady spot somewhere near your home. Turn the flowerpot upside down and prop it up on the rock.

After a few days, look inside the flowerpot. Draw pictures in your notebook of any creatures you find. Can you name them?

Bee home

Make this simple bee box and hang it in a sunny place outside. The straws should slope down into the bottle.

You will need
- Large plastic bottle
- Drinking straws
- Scissors
- String

Cut the top end off the bottle, and fill it with straws. Then tie string around the bottle and hang it outside.

Hamster funbox

Build a funbox

Your pet hamster or mouse will have lots of fun with this play box. It can climb in and out of it, as if on a climbing frame.

You will need
- Shoe box
- 4 cardboard tubes
- Poster paints
- Scissors
- Paint brush
- Pencil
- Cup

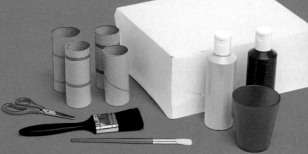

Position a cardboard tube in the middle of one end of the shoe box and draw round it. Repeat on the other sides of the box.

Make a hole in the centre of a circle and cut lines out to the edge of it. Then cut out the circle. Do this with all the circles on the box.

Mix some poster paint with a little water and carefully paint the cardboard box all over. Then leave the paint to dry.

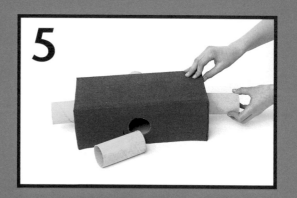

Paint the cardboard tubes a different colour. Paint one end of each tube and let it dry. Then paint the second half of the tube and leave that to dry too.

Push the cardboard tubes into the holes around the side of the box. They should fit firmly and stick out a bit. Now see if your hamster wants to play.

Glossary

Amphibian – an animal that is born in water but grows up to live on land as well

Ape – an animal that looks like a monkey without a tail

Bark – the outer layer of a tree's trunk or branches

Catkin – a spike of small, soft flowers on a tree

Chamber – a room

Cocoon – a wrapping that protects an animal

Colony – a group of animals that live together

Dam – a barrier built across a valley to hold back water

Den – a sheltered place where an animal lives

Enlarging – making bigger

Fungus – a plant, such as a toadstool, that grows on other plants

Galleries – long rooms or passages

Hibernate – to spend the whole winter in a deep sleep

Larva – a young insect that has just come out of its egg

Larvae – more than one larva

Mollusc – an animal with a soft body and a hard shell

Nectar – a liquid produced by flowers and collected by insects

Platform – a flat surface

Predator – an animal that hunts and eats other animals

Pregnant – going to have a baby

Prey – an animal that is hunted and killed by another animal

Roost – to settle down to sleep

Sea ice – ice that forms on the surface of the sea when it freezes

Shields – protects and looks after

Shredded – torn into strips

Snowdrift – a large heap of snow that has been piled up by the wind

Swarm – a large group of insects flying together

Parent and teacher notes

This book includes material that would be particularly useful in helping to teach children aged 7–11 elements of the English and Science curricula and some cross-curricular lessons, especially those involving Geography and Art.

Extension activities

Reading
Find all the words for an animal home used in this book. Can you say exactly what each word means?

Writing
There will be wild animals living near you, including birds, ants and bugs that live in gardens. Study one, and write about its home.

Look at the information about the trapdoor spider on page 15. Write a set of instructions telling it how to hunt for food. Can you write instructions for another animal in this book?

Make a poster with images of four different kinds of animal home. Add labels to show similarities and differences.

People are animals, too. Write a report about your home, explaining how it provides you and your family with shelter, warmth and protection.

There is information about hunting or avoiding predators on pages 6, 12, 14–15, 17, 24, 32 and 34. Write a newspaper-style article about an animal attack on another creature's home.

Write a poem about an animal's home, looking at it from the animal's point of view. Now write a poem from the point of view of a predator who wants to get to the animal inside the home!

Speaking and listening
Prepare a two-minute presentation about how different animals have adapted to their habitats.

Science

The topic relates to the scientific themes of growth and reproduction (pp6–7, 8–9, 11, 13, 15, 16–17, 18–19, 20–21, 27, 28–29, 32–33) habitats (throughout the book) and materials (pp6, 12, 14–15, 16, 18–19, 21, 22–23, 34, 36).

Cross-curricular links

Art and design: Draw a picture or make a collage showing an animal habitat. Can you include materials that the animal uses? Can you design an animal home for it?

Geography: Find the water habitats in this book. How are they different from each other? (See pages 8–9, 10–11, 32–33, 34–35).

This book mentions habitats in rainforests, deserts, snowy places and mountains. Find this information in the book and then use an atlas or the Internet to find out where in the world these habitats are found. Which is closest to where you live?

Using the projects

Children can follow or adapt these projects at home. Here are some ideas for extending them:

Page 40: Divide the things you see into groups, such as 'Animals with wings', 'Animals with feathers', etc. This is called classifying animals. How many legs do they have? How do they move? What do they eat?

Page 41: Create a realistic landscape as a setting for your nest. You could build a tree or bush with lots of twigs and branches, or create a landscape on the ground from rocks and grasses.

Pages 42–43: Can you change the design to make it lower, or to conceal two people? Make a chart to show how many different types of animal visit the habitat you are in.

Pages 46–47: Which parts of the box does your pet spend the most time in? Why?

Did you know?

- When a polar bear cub is born it cannot see or hear for about a month!

- A platypus can consume its own body weight in food in 24 hours!

- The female potter wasp stuffs her nest with dead spiders and caterpillars before sealing it shut with mud. The creatures provide food for her larvae when they hatch.

- The male satin bowerbird collects feathers, shells and other colourful bits and pieces to attract a female to its nest.

- The bee hummingbird makes its nest from spiders' webs and bark scraps!

- The roof of the nest of the hamerkop, an African bird, is so strong it can carry the weight of a human being!

- The largest wasps' nest on record was found in New Zealand and measured 3.6 metres long, with a diameter of 1.8 metres!

- Prairie dogs stand guard at the entrance to their burrows. When they spot danger they bark a warning so the other prairie dogs can rush in to safety.

- The cave swiftlet builds its nest with saliva. It can take up to two months to make!

- Termites are tiny but their mounds can be taller than a human!

- The desert tortoise spends more than nine-tenths of its life in a burrow.

- Some spiders in the Americas build their webs and join them to their neighbour's web. With one massive web, they can catch more prey.

- Kingfishers stab at the riverbank with their sharp beaks to make a tunnel to lay their eggs in.

- Tent-building bats make their homes out of large leaves. They nibble them along the centre so the leaf drops down around them, like a tent.

Animal homes quiz

The answers to these questions can all be found by looking back through the book. See how many you get right. You can check your answers on page 56.

1) How many eggs does a queen wasp lay in each cell of her nest?
   A – 3
   B – 1
   C – 2

2) What do marmots block their burrow entrance with?
   A – Grass and straw
   B – Rocks and soil
   C – Sand

3) Where does the white stork build its nest?
   A – In a tree
   B – On the ground
   C – On top of chimneys and houses

4) What does a tortoise do when it is in danger?
   A – Run away
   B – Roll over on to its back
   C – Pull its head and legs back into its shell

5) What is the name given to the place where termites look after their young?
   A – Baby galleries
   B – Nursery galleries
   C – Grub galleries

6) Where does a beaver live?
   A – A den
   B – A nest
   C – A lodge

7) How many nests can orang-utans build in one day?
   A – 5
   B – 2
   C – 1

8) How does the water spider survive underwater?
   A – It spins a web and makes an air bubble
   B – It comes up to the surface to breathe
   C – It gets oxygen from plants under the water

9) What shape is the cape weaver bird's nest?
   A – Square
   B – Round
   C – Oval

10) When do kit foxes hunt?
    A – In the daytime
    B – At night
    C – Both during the day and night

11) Where do male gorillas sleep?
    A – In a tree
    B – In a nest
    C – On the ground

12) What is a flying group of bees called?
    A – A hive
    B – A swarm
    C – A herd

Find out more

Books to read

Coral Reef (At Home in the Biome) by
 Louise and Richard Spilsbury,
 Wayland, 2017

Ask Dr K Fisher about Animals by Claire
 Llewellyn, Kingfisher, 2009

*Do Turtles Sleep in Treetops? A Book about
 Animal Homes (Animals All Around)* by
 Laura Purdie Salas, Picture Window
 Books, 2006

Home Makers (Amazing Nature) by Matt
 Turner, Heinemann Library, 2004

Places to visit

Chester Zoo
www.chesterzoo.org
Chester Zoo has over 7,000 animals and
400 different species, some of which
feature in this book. With spectacular
gardens and plants from around the
world, the zoo creates a natural habitat
for the special animals that live there.

The Highland Wildlife Park
www.highlandwildlifepark.org
The wildlife collection at The Highland
Wildlife Park is unique. It includes Scottish
wildlife and endangered animals from
the world's mountains and tundra.

Hunstanton Sea Life Sanctuary
www.visitsealife.com/Hunstanton
Norfolk's leading sea life rescue centre,
Hunstanton has otter and penguin
sanctuaries and a seal hospital. You
can also travel through the amazing
underwater tunnel to gaze at sharks,
and hold a crab or touch a starfish
in the interactive rockpool!

Melbourne Zoo
www.zoo.org.au/MelbourneZoo
View more than 300 animal species at
this wonderful zoo. You can meet the
animal keepers, take a walk around
the butterfly house and get up close
to your favourite animals in the Wild
Encounters programme.

RSPB Ynys-hir Nature Reserve
*www.rspb.org.uk/reserves/guide/y/ynys-
hir/index.aspx*
Look out for birds of prey from one of the
nature hides, or spot some of the wading
birds and butterflies at this reserve.
Follow the brass rubbing trail, go on
a dragons and damsels walk or have
a teddy bears' picnic!

Websites

www.bbc.co.uk/nature/animals
Find out all you need to know about
your favourite animals on this website.
You can learn about their habitats,
what they eat and how they survive.

*http://kids.nationalgeographic.com/kids/
animals*
This website is crammed full of
fascinating facts, fun games and
hilarious animal photographs.

*http://www.activewild.com/australian-
animals-list*
Find out everything you need to know
about Australian animals. You can learn
some amazing animal facts and join the
newsletter list.

Animal homes quiz answers

1) B
2) B
3) C
4) C
5) B
6) C
7) B
8) A
9) C
10) B
11) C
12) B